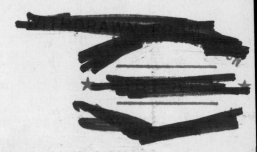

The Life of Ibsen

VOLUME TWO

HENRIK IBSEN

Painting by Eilif Peterssen

THE LIFE OF
IBSEN

Halvdan Koht

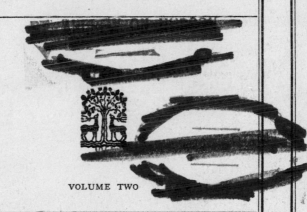

VOLUME TWO

THE AMERICAN-SCANDINAVIAN FOUNDATION

W · W · NORTON & COMPANY, INC., PUBLISHERS

NEW YORK

Contents

Illustrations

Chapter One

IBSEN AND NORWAY

IBSEN once said that when he left home in 1864 he went "into exile." About the time that he wrote these words in a letter (1870) he expressed the same feeling in a poem, a revision of the verses entitled "The Eider Duck," which he had written in his youth. When at that time (1851) he described man's ruthless robbery of the eider duck's nest, he had no suggestion of remedy or hope for the bird:

> *Then feels the bird that his hope is lost,*
> *Then a bleeding breast is all he owns,*
> *Then pines he to death on a lonely coast.*

And it was thus with man too; as the dreams with which he had warmed his heart were plucked away from him, all courage must depart, and eternal night would come into his soul. But now, twenty years later, Ibsen had found a way of escape for the bird as well as for himself:

> *But steal this treasure, his third, his last—*
> *One night he spreads his wings to the blast;*
>
> *With bleeding bosom the sea-fog dun*
> *He cleaves, to the South, to the South and sun!*

Ibsen had been forced to give up his dreams; and he could no longer remain at home. Everything there seemed to repel him, and to rob him of courage and will. To save his life, to save himself, he had to get away.

"I had to escape from the swinishness up there," he wrote in a letter from Rome two years after his departure, "to be fairly cleansed. There I never could preserve any wholeness of inner life; wherefore I was one thing in my production and quite another thing outside of it—wherefore, also, my production was not whole."

A year later he wrote to his mother-in-law, Fru Magdalene Thoresen: "I am often unable to comprehend how you can endure it up there! Life there, as it now appears to me, has something unspeakably wearing about it; it wears the spirit out of one's being, wears the energy out of one's will. It is the curse of narrow circumstances that they make the soul narrow."

The narrowness at home was, so to speak, both physical and spiritual. There was dearth of great thoughts and wholeness of will; everything had to give way to the petty material considerations of everyday life. There was no spontaneous enjoyment of art and poetry. The community was so small and cramped that people were continually elbowing each other. Ibsen had felt it altogether too poignantly at the time he published Love's Comedy, how small town gossip confounded writing and life. Yet the worst hindrance, perhaps, lay in the many friends by whom one was surrounded and to whom one had to accommodate one's self.

"Friends are a costly luxury," he wrote to Georg Brandes in 1870; "and if one's capital consists in a calling and a mission in life, one cannot afford to keep friends. The expenditure in keeping friends does not, to be sure, consist in what one does for them, but in what one, out of consideration for them, re-frains from doing, whereby many a spiritual growth is crippled within one. I have experienced it, and therefore I have to look back on several years during which I could not attain to being myself."

Ibsen found great difficulty in speaking out freely and openly, especially perhaps with his best friends. It grieved him; he never felt that he could stand undivided and true before them, as he wished to do. He was shy; he could not lay bare his soul in the presence of others. And thus, though unwillingly, he took on the tone of his associates. "I understand clearly," he once wrote, "that it is really only in the solitude of my own thoughts that I am myself."

Therefore he had to live far away, and to be by himself. It was not because Norway happened to be narrow and small, but because it was his home. No matter where he had lived in the world, his home would have been a prison and a peril to him. He could not be free before he got away.

There were enough people who wished to call him back again. Only three months after he had gone away, he received an offer of the director's position at the Christiania Theater. But he declined promptly and decisively, although the position would have given him an assured livelihood; and each time the offer was repeated, in 1870 and in 1884, he put it aside with equal promptness. He admitted that there was in the thought of the theater something that drew him, something that awakened long-ing and unrest in his mind; but he started back apprehensively—he was afraid. "The point is," he wrote as late as in 1884, "that I could not write freely and unreservedly and fully up there, which is the same as saying that I could not write at all."

He had set out with the thought of remaining away for a year or two. After nine months had passed, he wrote Björnson a letter which never reached its destination, a circumstance for which he was later thankful; for the letter, he admitted, was written in an uncharitable and bitter tone against his own country, and in it he had declared that he wished never to go home again. But some weeks later he wrote: "After all, I must go home"; and the same thought was repeated at the end of two years. However, he continued to shrink from it, and delayed his return year after year.

At the mere thought of home, he was filled with misgivings. He expressed something of himself in the words which Brand uttered as he viewed again the neighborhood of his childhood:

> *As I near my home, I change,*
> *To my very self grow strange—*
> *Wake, as baffled Samson woke,*
> *Shorn and fetter'd, tamed and broke.*

He seemed to feel a sort of numbness; he lost his strength and courage, and could not keep a hold on his great thoughts and dreams.

At various times, particularly in 1866, he thought of settling in Copenhagen and establishing his home there, feeling for a time that this was perhaps "the true center of Scandinavian life, least fettered by the prevailing prejudices." But he grew less and less inclined to take up his abode there. Copenhagen was not home, and yet it was not sufficiently foreign. He feared that there, too, he would be too closely pressed between friends and enemies. He was aware of the constraint upon Georg Brandes there early in the seventies, and he began to fear that the atmosphere of Copenhagen would prove to be as suffocating as that of Norway.

His choice, then, was between Oslo and countries quite foreign. The thought that sooner or later he must go home was like a nightmare to him. Outward circumstances, particularly concern for the education and training of his son, might impel him to return, but he constantly resisted the thought. Even in so foreign a country as Germany he felt that he was restrained and checked by the society about him. "What will it be, then, when I finally reach home!"

"I hardly understand," he wrote in 1868, "how it will be possible to live outside of Italy, and least of all how it will be possible to live in Christiania. But clearly it must be done. I feel, meanwhile, that one must isolate one's self there—at least that I must do so if I shall not make enemies of half the people." He repeated the thought in the following year: "It is not possible for an author to live there unless he is able coldly to decline all party affiliation and to assume a position of independence."

On the other hand, he was forever laying plans for a visit to Norway, and almost every year we hear of an intended trip home. But even this was delayed. The mere thought of a winter in Norway frightened him: "Either I should within a month have made all the people there my enemies, or I should again slip into all sorts of disguisements and become a lie both to myself and to others."

He was in Sweden in 1869, and in Denmark in 1870. But to Norway he did not venture before 1874, and then the visit gave him no taste for more. The sense of aversion remained in him even ten years later: "Ten years ago when, after an absence of another ten years, I sailed up the fjord, I literally felt my breast tighten with a sense of oppression and faintness. The same thing was true of my stay there; I was no longer myself among all those cold and uncomprehending Norwegian eyes in the windows and on the streets."

Thus he was more than ever held off by fear and more strongly than ever impressed by the thought that he could not permanently thrive or work in Norway. This time he waited eleven years before he returned for another visit.

This does not by any means indicate that he severed all connection with his native land. Thoughts of doing such a thing had indeed arisen in him while the question of a government stipend was being considered, in 1863 and in 1866. At various times later, too, his anger flared up, and he threatened to make himself a foreigner. Thus in 1871, when the printer who during the fifties had charge of *Illustreret Nyhedsblad* took it into his head to reprint *The Vikings at Helgeland,* announcing besides that he intended to reprint also *Lady Inger of Östråt,* Ibsen became wild with anger at this "intended raid on my purse"; and as the printer would not yield, a lawsuit followed. When the author's friend, M. Birkeland, ventured to hint that the question of legality might be doubtful, Ibsen was beside himself with rage. "Here I sat," he wrote home, "in happy peace of mind, working on my new drama. From Sweden, from Denmark, and from my surroundings here, I experience only things that must give me joy; but from Norway every ill fortune seems to come upon me. What do those people want? Am I not sufficiently far away?" Then the thought darted into his mind that he wished to part company with such people: "This is to me a matter of great importance; for if Jensen's plan of spoliation should win sympathy and support at home, it is my intention, come what may, to sever all connection with Norway and never again set my foot there."

However, his anger soon cooled; in about two months he again wrote about visiting Norway. And as he won his case against the printer in both the city court and the supreme court, he had proof that the country would protect his rights. These fits of anger left no permanent traces, except in so far as they helped to keep alive in his thought both his native country and his indignation. But both of these were conditions for his writing.

He had been able to sever all connection with his parental home, for he felt no spiritual relationship with it; but in the larger home, his native land, he was so firmly rooted that it would have been spiritual death for him to break away from it. He had his own work in mind when he let Brand say:

"To a man's feet his native haunt
   Is as unto the tree the root.
   If there his labor fill no want,
   His deeds are doomed, his music mute."

Brand had to remain at home and fight his battle there. Any other action appeared to him as a desertion. Ibsen had felt the same thing in 1862 when, writing about the actors at the Norwegian theater, he said that they had better endure hunger and privation than desert their calling.

It is clear from what he wrote at the time that he believed other artists, such as poets, might leave home and yet not shirk their duty toward the fatherland; that, indeed, it might be neces-

logs and trees. The bridge shook, and people fled; but Ibsen remained standing, to watch and remember, for thus he had stood in boyhood and gazed down into the rapids of the Skien river. A stranger stopped beside him, and Ibsen was so absorbed in his thoughts of home that he began to speak to the stranger—in Norwegian. The stranger proved to be an Englishman, and afterwards the conversation was carried on in French. But the content of Ibsen's words was how everything repeats itself and how memories become dreams. It was Norway that had awakened in him.

In a way, his home was always with him. When, in completing his collection of poems in 1871, he came to view his entire career as a poet, he gave his homesickness the form of verse in the little poem "Burnt Ships." He had turned his ships southward, leaving the snow for summer and sunshine. He had even burned his ships, so that only the smoke blowing northward made a bridge between himself and his homeland; and yet

> From the sun-warmed lowland
> Each night that betides,
> To the huts of the snow-land
> A horseman rides.

Dreams and memories turned homeward. And it was remarkable how recollections of youth and childhood appeared in his writings, much more now than ever before—Skien in *The League of Youth*, Grimstad in *Pillars of Society*, and many, many other memories in other places. We must oftentimes wonder at the way in which everything he had seen during his boyhood, when he sat musing and seemed to live in a world

by himself, was engraved in his brain as in a film. His great
ability to *see* became really evident now that these things returned in his writings, and the truth is that the more he used
these memories of home, the richer and more vital his writing
became.

In speaking of his work, he invariably said that the thing
which counted with him, the thing that he always struggled with
and worked toward, was to see each one of his characters vividly
before his eyes. He must know them through and through, so
that he was not only familiar with what they thought, but so
that he heard how they spoke, saw how they walked, and stood,
and were dressed. Every button in their clothing must be visible
to him. But if all this should be true, the characters must neces-
sarily be Norwegian; otherwise he could not know them thoroughly, could not make them speak naturally. And it seemed to
himself that their very temperament must be ultra-Norwegian.

In 1886, when he had published *Rosmersholm*, a German
friend said to him that there was something unfamiliar in the
book, something which a German could never fully understand.
"Yes," cried Ibsen, much more animated than he usually was.
"You are right about that. I comprehend. The people up there
are indeed different from you here, and he who would know
me fully, must know Norway. The grand but austere nature
with which people are surrounded in the North, the lonely,
isolated life—their homes often lie many miles apart—compel
them to be indifferent to other people, and to care only about
their own concerns; therefore they become ruminative and
serious-minded; they ponder and doubt; and they often despair.

With us every other man is a philosopher! Then there are the long, dark winters, with the thick fog about the houses— Oh, they long for the sun!"

It was a part of his own temperament that he thus described and tried to explain, and the explanation was neither particularly original nor deeply striking. But it shows how intimately he felt himself to be rooted in Norwegian nature and life and racial temperament. That was where his mental life grew and found nourishment. It was always on Norwegian society, Norwegian thought, and Norwegian questions that his works were built; they could not have been possible without this foundation. When he had roamed about for more than six years, he still said in a letter: "But I feel more Norwegian at heart than I have ever done before."

There was something almost clairvoyant in the way he followed events at home. He associated with but few aside from Scandinavians while he lived among strangers, and he felt that something was lacking when he could not meet with Scandinavians; but many a time, too, he led quite a lonely existence, and it was largely a matter of chance if he met anyone from whom he could hear news. He corresponded but little with people at home, and months might pass without a word from Norway. But he could not bear it for too long a time. "It is intolerable for any great length of time to be outside of all communication with home," he once wrote in 1868, after having spent two months in traveling without receiving any mail. Of Norwegian newspapers he seldom read more than a single one— during the first ten or twelve years it was *Morgenbladet*—and sometimes one Danish paper besides. But he read his newspapers with an avidity which was quite unusual, searching them through from beginning to end, advertisements and all, and devouring every word. In the same way he utilized people who came from home, letting them talk and relate, while he listened with undivided attention. Thus he was informed about everything, and sensed every movement of life at home.

Perhaps he understood and interpreted everything in the light of memories of the youthful years that he had spent there. He did not always comprehend the great new forces which arose in Norwegian society and made it over. But in the light of his own memory, things were given exactly such form as served to kindle fire and life in his own soul.

It is clear enough that life in strange lands gave him many kinds of knowledge and left deep imprints in him. He himself was well aware that "the soil has much to do with the forms within which the imagination works creatively." When he thought back upon *Brand* and *Peer Gynt*, his first works from Italy, he felt that he could say with one of the characters in Ludvig Holberg: "See, this was an intoxication of wine." And in *The League of Youth*, his first work from Germany, he thought there was something reminiscent of "Knackwurst und Bier." He noticed also that German philosophy and politics broadened his outlook on the world.

But he never became what in German is called *eingebürgert*, spiritually at home, in any of the foreign countries—Germany or Italy—in which he lived. Here, too, he found it necessary to isolate himself if he would be free. It may be a question if he ever, as long as he was abroad, became thoroughly familiar with ways of living and thinking in the foreign communities. But the foreign country at least gave an opportunity for comparison, and as he observed life and events there, everything at home seemed still smaller and paltrier, and his anger could burn still hotter.

Foreigners who know Norway only through Ibsen's works often judge our country by the pictures he gives in them. But this is unfair; for it is not objective portrayal, it is polemical writing he has given us; and the strongest evidence of what Norway was, is perhaps after all the fact that Ibsen felt so bound to it. All of his writing was directed against his homeland. If this land had not given him the "gift of sorrow," for which he had so often asked, it had at least given him an abundance of "the gift of anger," and he felt, as did Brand, that here, toward this people, "The true, the sovereign Love—is Hate!" Yet his hatred was love. More than once he grasped an opportunity to assure his countrymen that he did not at all hate Norway or everything Norwegian: "It is the excrescences upon our social life, that I abhor." But of these excrescences he found enough to raise his anger, and his writings grew from them.

Once, in 1873, a German critic called Ibsen's poem, "Signals of the North," a *Hohngedicht* against Germany. But Ibsen instantly protested: "There are altogether too many things at home, in our own lands, which I find it necessary to mock, to permit me to take upon myself the trouble of mocking the Germans."

He remained always a Norwegian poet, and could not be anything else. For it was Norway that added fuel to the flame of his anger. It was to this he gave expression in the greeting that he sent home for the millennial festival in 1872:

My people, who in bowlfuls deep have given
The wholesome-bitter, strengthening drink whereby,
Near to my waiting grave, as poet I
Took strength to fight 'mid broken rays of even,
Ye who gave exile-staff and ever-nigh
Knapsack of sorrows, shoes for one care-driven—
Ye who have all this solemn burden lent me,
Greeting I give from lands where ye have sent me.

I greet ye, thanking unintended merit
That purified my soul through painful moil;
All thriving in the garden of my spirit
Has still its root within my homeland soil.
If here their growth is rich and full and easy,
The cause lies in your weather, gray and breezy.
What sun-heat loosened, first in mist was living.
Homeland, have thanks, my best remains your giving.

Chapter Two

PEER THE NORWEGIAN

IT was a new face which thus appeared in the Scandinavian world of letters—a man who drew poetry from new well-springs. To many there seemed to be something strange about him, which caused them to draw back; but to a larger and larger number, and especially to the youth of his day, he had an appeal greater than that of almost any other man.

Early in 1867 (January 27 and February 3) the Danish *Illustreret Tidende* published a full account of Ibsen's life, written by the journalist A. Falkman. It was the first time that a connected story of his work had been presented to Danish readers. Here it was pointed out how the new Norwegian authors, and especially Ibsen, must attract the youth of Denmark; for they revealed an ethical principle in their writing in contrast to the æstheticism of the older Danish writers, which people were now growing tired of.

The thing that in this connection especially characterized Ibsen was pointed out by Georg Brandes in a critical treatise in the *Dansk Maanedsskrift* the same fall, the first attempt to penetrate into the spiritual groundwork of Ibsen's writings. Brandes saw that the vital principle in him was his burning ethical indignation, his hatred of all deceit and hypocrisy: "Greatness and strength, of the passions and of the will, and of the will that is inspired by passion, that is the ideal of this author."

Brandes, however, was still so bound by old literary conventions that he could not regard the drama of indignation as true art. He praised with understanding and joy all the rich poetic art of *The Pretenders;* but he thought that in *Brand* Ibsen had strayed from the right way. "Therefore," he said in concluding his article, "it is necessary that he leave the direction he has taken in *Love's Comedy* and *Brand*. Unfortunately there is no doubt that it will be difficult for him to do so; but . . . he is too much of an artist to fail in the long run to see what is poetry and what is not."

The next year, when Brandes reprinted this treatise in his *Studies in Æstheticism*, he was forced to delete the last statement. The new drama which Ibsen had just then published destroyed his hopes; it did not conform to Brandes's literary demands, but continued in Ibsen's own way. This drama was *Peer Gynt*.

"After *Brand*, *Peer Gynt* followed almost as of itself," wrote Ibsen two years later. Thus it seemed to him then, and there was an inner truth in the statement. But as a matter of fact the drama did not come quite of itself.

When he had completed *Brand*, Ibsen first thought of going back to the work for which he had made plans before he set out from Norway, the drama about Magnus Heineson. For many months he struggled with the plan, but though it seemed to himself to be "full-grown" within him, nothing came of it. In the spring of 1866, in May, we hear that he was more and more inclined to begin the drama of Julian instead. The subject had then been in his mind for more than two years, and it interested and attracted him more and more strongly.

During four summer months of this year, from June to September, he again lived in one of the small towns in the Alban hills, this time Frascati. He had rooms in one of the old castles there, Palazzo Grazioli, and had in his immediate neighborhood remainders of the classic age, namely, the country house and theater of Cicero. From his workroom he had a broad view of the Roman Campagna with mountains round about; he thought he saw before him "the field on which the world's history has presented its greatest battle." These must be favorable surroundings for the development of a drama about Julian, and it must have been to this work he referred when he told Botten-Hansen late in July: "Now I shall soon begin to write in earnest; I still go about wrestling with the material, but I know that I shall soon have the beast under my control, and the rest will come of itself."

But it did not come of itself. Instead he began, toward the close of August, a work of an entirely different kind: he went back to *Love's Comedy* and began revising it for a new edition. Hegel was at once willing to publish it. Ibsen thought that "the language must be purified" first, and he used the month of September for this work. The purifying consisted in taking out all the ultra-Norwegian words in the play, in order to make it more acceptable for Danish readers.

It was at this time he received notice that the Norwegian government had granted him a new traveling stipend, and when he returned to Rome in the beginning of October, after completing the revision of *Love's Comedy*, he made plans to go to Hellas and to Paris. He clearly had the intention of doing preparatory work for the drama about Julian.

A month later, however, on November 2, he wrote to Hegel that he was uncertain what he would first begin to write: "I have yet another subject or two in mind; but this very dispersion in my interest shows that none of them is yet sufficiently ripe; however, I feel with certainty that the ripening will soon be accomplished, and hope that sometime in the spring I shall be able to submit to you the finished manuscript."

These words are, I believe, the first indication that a new subject matter was awakening within him—that which later became *Peer Gynt*. But what was the reason that this new subject was born within him and *Brand* thus received its natural sequel?

It was surely no accident that during the last summer he had taken up again *Love's Comedy*. He informed Hegel that this drama could be "regarded as a forerunner" of *Brand*, and we have evidence here that the mood which had created these two plays was still present in him. Moreover, the preface which he wrote for the second edition of *Love's Comedy* contained a sharp polemic thrust at Norway, ridiculing the "sound realism" which made the Norwegians settle down smugly in existing conditions and not brook anything that might disturb them.

When he struck out from the drama everything that was characteristically Norwegian, he did so not only with a desire to please Danish readers, but also as a means of expressing the anger and contempt with which he regarded the Norwegians. He seemed to have discovered that there was no vestige of truth in the national boasting at home, and he was heartily tired of everything that bore the name of nationalism. Especially he turned away from the campaign for a purely Norwegian language, which in his mind became a symbol of affected and un-

true national consciousness. For his own part, he had during the
past years gone a good deal farther toward making his language
ultra-Norwegian than was wholly natural to him, and now he
reversed his position so completely that he even came to hate
the language movement.

During the winter of 1866–67 the young Norwegian vernacular writer, Kristofer Janson, was in Rome, and his partici-
pation in the Christmas festival at the Scandinavian Club threatened seriously to create a scandal; for he had hinted that he
would make his contribution to the entertainment by reading one
of his own vernacular stories, and Ibsen had made it known that
in such an event he would leave the party. All through the eve-
ning, therefore, everyone sat dreading what would happen. This
lasted so long that finally all thought Janson had given up his
plan. But suddenly his voice was heard saying that, instead of
reading anything of his own, he would tell the story "A Dangerous Courting" (*Ei Fårleg Friing*) by Björnson. This he did, in
his bright and melodious language. It was so attractive that
Ibsen forgot his anger and stayed to listen, and everything
turned out well. But we know that at bottom he was not pleased.
Far from it. And he often entered upon heated arguments with
Janson on the language question. On one occasion he became so
angry that he threw a chair after his opponent with the exclama-
tion, "You confounded *stril!*" [1] The matter was made still worse
when his wife took sides with Janson. "Yes, of course," cried
Ibsen, "you, too, are a stril!"

Those who associated with him in Rome at this time often

---

[1] *Stril* is the nickname applied by the people of Bergen to the fishermen and
peasants in the surrounding country.

both saw and felt his bad humor. One might have expected that the great success of *Brand* would have moderated the anger within him. But sufficient time had not yet passed since he was fairly bursting with anger, and he did not readily forget. He was still nursing the vexation he had gone through at the time when he published *Love's Comedy,* and even late in 1867 he bridled at the memory of how the comic paper *Vikingen* had made sport of him more than four years earlier. He called it being "slandered" in a "scurrilous paper." With equal care he nursed his political anger. We are told that in 1867 he would become white with anger when he spoke of how the Germans had treated Denmark, and of how Norway and Sweden had deserted the Danes. His own countrymen he never designated by any other name than "the scoundrels." He hated the Swedes for the slackness of their politics, which harmonized so poorly with their boasting of Gustavus Adolphus and Charles XII. "Keep still, you make me sick!" he cried, striking the table, if anyone tried to say a good word for them. And as late as in 1868 he wrote that the worst thing at home was the "flirtation with the Swedes."

He now lived in far better circumstances than during his first two years in Rome. During that time he had too often been compelled to wear threadbare clothes with holes under his coat-sleeves, and though he pretended not to care, he had been distressed by the fact that his poverty was thus evident to all. Now he could buy fine clothes and attire himself in proper style. Yet he felt a need to guard his social standing, and was always afraid that someone should slight him. If anything occurred that might be interpreted to mean that he or his household were not given the same consideration as others—if, for instance, something went wrong with an invitation—he flared up and would not let the offense pass unreproved. His pride was developed in an excessive degree. At a certain banquet in the Scandinavian Club someone proposed a toast to the committee that had looked after the food and wine. It happened to be Ibsen and another man; but Ibsen rose and, stamping his foot on the floor, said: "My health shall not be drunk on the ground that I am a member of the food committee."

It was but natural that he should know his own worth. He had struggled so long to find himself that it must give a sense of exaltation to get the measure of his own ability. Yet the feeling was so new that it brought insecurity and led to exaggeration. With perfect seriousness he would speak to one of his friends in Rome about how he would remain down there and "dictate to them all at home." He often said that he did not write only for the immediate future, but for all eternity, and when one of his friends answered him by remarking that in a thousand years even the greatest men would probably be forgotten, Ibsen was quite beside himself: "Get away from me with your metaphysics. If you rob me of eternity, you rob me of everything." He was in constant apprehension of anything that might terminate his work as a writer, such as illness or accident. Therefore he never ventured out on dangerous mountain or boat trips, and it was not merely in fun when he said: "What if a tile should land on one's head!"

He was especially sensitive after drinking a pint or more of wine. Then his irritability would often break out at almost nothing, and people who were entirely innocent were sometimes made to suffer. But even at such times there was evident in him an underlying need for warmth and love. If, in a group of boon companions, he had heaped abuse upon some poor wretch, he would probably follow this by speaking gently and kindly of one who stood in need of it. On one occasion, when he had vented his wrath by pitilessly teasing a great dog inside an openwork gate, his eyes fell suddenly on two small children who had approached, and—so one of those who were present relates— "with a surprising expression of kindness and good will in his eyes he took between two of his fingers a bit of the girl's cheek— a caress which revealed both human kindliness and a desire to protect. It was an adagio after the storm."

To the man who related this, Ibsen wrote some years later that these days were his "Roman *Sturm-und-Drang* period"; and the same man has described the effect of Ibsen's inconsistencies on his associates: "His high ideals, his great pettiness in everyday matters, his joy over Italy and art, his residue of bitterness against Norway, his recently past pecuniary difficulties, and the secret desire to exert power, these things and many others that moved within him, caused him to explode in one direction or the other, and he went about among the Scandinavians like a lion whom most people were rather afraid of."

After thus following Ibsen's life in Rome during the first year after the publication of *Brand,* one can easily understand his laying aside all historical topics to devote himself instead to a continuation of the literature of indignation and chastisement begun in *Brand.* Yet his anger now was expressed in an altogether different form. Angry and impatient though he continued to be, he was now farther removed from the things that had worked so powerfully on him and roused his fury. He no longer went about merely seeing red. There was going on within his spirit a transformation of a kind that is not uncommon.

It is often true that, even when the hottest flame of anger subsides, the agitation it has roused in the soul does not therefore die down. On the contrary, anger sets in motion abilities and powers which may otherwise lie bound or dormant deep within us. Anger releases and awakens a new desire for mental activity. It becomes a creative power because it breaks through old inhibitions; he who is quiet becomes lively, he who is timid becomes brave, and all the energies of the spirit are set vibrating more rapidly.

It was exactly this that happened to Ibsen. In *Brand* he had created a chastiser of the hypocrisy and the spirit of compromise in the Norwegian people, and thus set up the exact opposite of the Danish *Adam Homo*, but now he began to laugh at the pettiness of his people, and became desirous to create the Norwegian counterpart to the Danish "Adam," the Norwegian Peer, at once a type and a caricature of his people. He would no longer thunder and scold, but mock and ridicule. It was Ibsen's laughter that found an outlet.

This laughter had been heard often in *Love's Comedy*, and even in *Brand* it had not been entirely absent. One need only recall the manner in which the Dean is portrayed in the last act, to detect that Ibsen has been secretly laughing as he wrote. But only in *Peer Gynt* was his laughter given free rein. Here, too, there are times when his wrath appears stark and bitter; but for the most part it is transfused with the bold and wanton joy that comes of feeling that strength wells up within one. Not in pain this time, but in delight, the poet plied his whip.

How did he find the "hero" who was to personify all the hollow boasting which he thought characterized the Norwegians? The type was suggested in Norwegian folk legends, and it was not difficult for Ibsen, the collector of legends, to discover him. Perhaps he had heard of him directly while traveling in Gudbrandsdalen. At any rate the man was named and described in Asbjörnsen's *Norwegian Fairy Tales and Folk Legends* in the collection of 1847, which just now, at the close of 1866, appeared in a new edition. A certain man of Sel, Anders Ulvsvollen, had told Asbjörnsen about him: "That Peer Gynt was a queer fellow," said Anders. "He was a spinner of yarns and a teller of tales that certainly would have amused you. He always claimed that he himself had taken part in all the stories which people said had happened in olden days."

Ibsen found it amusing that such a person should be an historical character; and according to Asbjörnsen he was said to have lived only two or three generations ago. Later research has attempted to show that the true Peer Gynt lived as far back as in the seventeenth century; but there is at least nothing historical in what the folk legends have told about him.

Whatever may or may not be true of the historical Peer Gynt, he was but the small theme about which Ibsen built his rich imaginative structure. The legends about Peer Gynt were but ordinary romantic stories and fairy tales, the only thing that stood out as peculiar to them being the story of the great *Boyg* of Atnedalen, an incident which did become a main symbol for

Ibsen, and which was among the things that nourished his creative imagination. At bottom he was glad that the sources did not give too much information about Peer. "I did not have much to build my drama on," he wrote to Hegel, "but I have had all the more freedom in my work." Around the Gudbrandsdal hunter, Peer Gynt, he gathered, one after another, the characteristics of the Norwegian racial temperament, thus re-making him into the truly Norwegian Peer.

The thing that seemed to him the fundamental characteristic in this genuine Norwegian was the damnable impulse to lie his way out of the demands and difficulties of life, a characteristic which Ibsen hated from the bottom of his heart. But the thing that explained and indeed gave something of expiation to the lie, was the riotous imagination from which it grew up, an imagination which one might laugh at and which one was almost compelled to like.

The character of the Norwegian Peer, therefore, became altogether different from that of the Danish Adam Homo, not at all the prosaic everyday temperament of the Dane, not merely a low and mean charlatan, but a wanton madcap of a poet, a fellow who at least could dream greatly, and who had sufficient ability for achievement, but who constantly lost himself in flights of fancy.

It was Ibsen's own character that was reflected in this man. He had so often dreamed that he would do something really great, had perhaps spoken of it, too. He thought that he had in him the qualities of intellectual leadership; but year after year had slipped away from him, and he had noticed how people sneered and whispered behind his back until it scorched his very being. He had wished that he might go about unseen, or he had tried to deaden the pain with something "strong"; for he himself could not get beyond mere talk.

Recently, while writing *Brand*, he had felt as if he were taking part in strife and action, and there had been a sense of jubilation within him. Writing this drama gave an outlet to the thoughts that tormented his soul. Now, afterwards, it seemed to him that he had merely evaded the struggle and the call to action; it appeared to him, as he wrote in a letter, that *Brand* was "wholly and thoroughly an æsthetic work without a trace of anything else." He had written a drama, not performed a deed. *"Brand,"* Arne Garborg once wrote, "is ideally what Kierkegaard wanted the man of his day to be in reality. Herein lies the way of escape. The absolute ethical demand is translated into æstheticism; thereby its sting is broken." But the sting remained in Ibsen, and tormented him. Therefore he again felt the desire to search and chastise himself; and it was by means of self-dissection that he created Peer Gynt.

He admitted this openly in a speech in 1874, in which he gave an account of what he had written during the last ten years: everything had been lived through within him. He had, for instance in *Brand*, built on things great and fair, to which his soul in its strongest moments had attained. But he had also written of the opposite things, which to his own eyes must appear as dregs and grounds in his soul. "Indeed, gentlemen," he said, "no one can artistically represent that for which he has not to a certain extent, and at least on some occasions, found the model in himself. And where is the man among us who has not now and then felt and recognized in himself a contradiction be-

tween words and actions, between will and task, between life
and teaching? And who among us has not, at least on certain occasions, been egoistically sufficient unto himself, and, half apprehensively and half in good faith, has glossed over his attitude,
both in his own eyes and in those of others?" He might as well
have said, quoting his own play:

> *Blood's never so thin as all that;*
> *One cannot but feel one's akin to Peer Gynt.*

Once, fifteen years earlier, he had created a character who
thus evaded the seriousness of life and made of it a mere play
of words and imagination. It was the romantic poet, Julian Paul-
sen in *St. John's Night*. Ibsen had written from without rather
than from within this Julian, and had portrayed him satirically.
Now the feeling that he shared responsibility and blame forced
itself upon him. It was even more evident in the first version of
the new drama than in the final form—in such lines as these:

> *There is something unpleasant, a mystery*
> *In the sharing of responsibility.*

In this first version we are also given more clearly to understand what kind of responsibility it was that weighed upon him.
It was exactly the thing of which he had complained two years
earlier in the poem "To the Partners in Guilt"—the self-delusion
of national romanticism. Therefore the great feast in the hall
of the mountain king was first opened by all the trolls singing
"For Norway, the Birthplace of Heroes." Ibsen had himself
enjoyed this song. It was one of the few that he knew, and year
after year he had written poems to the same tune, songs in
memory of the forefathers, for the Seventeenth of May, and for
other festivals. In *Andhrimner* (1851) he had dealt severely

with the "national tinsel finery" of the musical drama *The Home
of the Fairy,* which found its climax in the old boastful song.
Now he chastised himself for the sins of the intervening period
by making the song a symbol of the most narrow-minded
nationalism.

He had other sins to confess. It seemed to him now that he
had never viewed life with the proper seriousness, that he had
always "gone roundabout." There might be something of worth
in such evasion, too; he remembered things from his Grimstad
days that had left stains in his soul, making him feel "befouled
and disgraced." [2] It was not only fear that afterwards held him
back—it seemed a sacrilege to "Go in with that troll-rabble after
me still." Yet he knew that it was true as Brand had said:

*"Though you give all, and life retain,
I tell you that your gift is vain."*

Now he made it Peer Gynt's worst failing that he fled from
responsibility and obeyed the command of the Boyg: "Go roundabout."

While Ibsen thus dissected himself, while Peer Gynt grad-
ually took living shape in his mind, memory after memory arose
within him and added trait upon trait to the new dramatic creation.

He remembered his father, old Knud Ibsen of Skien, whose
wild speculations and uncontrolled spending when the times
seemed favorable, had been the very first experience that life

[2] I may mention a detail which perhaps gives quite external evidence that
his thoughts went back thither. The poor fellow, Mads Moen, from whom
Peer Gynt in the drama steals the bride, has been given the name of a sheriff
in one of the western Nedenes districts, about 1840. It is possible that this
was the very sheriff who collected the moneys for the support of the son born
to Ibsen there.

had given him of how the imagination may overpower judgment and the sense of reality. He made of Peer Gynt's father an equally reckless and light-hearted speculator.

He remembered his mother, Marichen Ibsen, whom, according to his own testimony, he portrayed in Åse, the mother of Peer Gynt, certainly "with necessary exaggerations." In reality we know nothing of his mother that corresponds wholly with the temperament of Åse; it is chiefly the never-failing love of motherhood that forms the bond between them. Yet there may be an underlying memory from childhood in the fact that Ibsen lets Peer Gynt relate how his mother sat by the bedside "and sang many a lilt and lay" and played at fairy tales with him. Perhaps Ibsen in his childhood had likewise been nourished by fairy tales and rhymes.

He remembered the great dreamer and restless experimenter who had once taken him into the service of national romanticism, Ole Bull. As soon as Bull had the Norwegian Theater in Bergen well started, he left it for a new undertaking; in the spring of 1852 he had gone to America to found a Norwegian ideal community there, Oleana. Ditmar Meidell has described with gay exaggeration the Eldorado dreams aroused by Ole Bull in those who wished to accompany him; and the well-known song about "Oleana" has kept the memory alive down to our own times. The outcome was sad enough; Ole Bull expended all his means, and his colony was a total failure. Ibsen clearly had this ill-founded experiment in mind when he let Peer Gynt dream of his empire, "Gyntiana." There can be no doubt that the national visionary, Ole Bull, helped to contribute material for Peer the Norwegian.

In addition, there appeared to Ibsen's memory a visionary of an altogether different sort, a politician and member of the Storthing who had been an inexhaustible source of fun to all the *Andhrimner*-friends in 1851, and especially gratifying to the ironic sense of A. O. Vinje—the lawyer F. G. Lerche, radical and national, yet not a dreamer like Ole Bull, but a man who involuntarily took the products of his own brain to be truth itself. It was of him Vinje said that he made "stating the facts" another term for "lying"; and just therein lay his quality of genius. He told the truth, but "in a free artistic translation" so that it was entirely transformed. This characteristic of his harmonized wonderfully well with the Peer Gynt of the legends.

At the same time Ibsen was thinking of A. O. Vinje himself—not the sensitive, double-visioned doubter, but the irrepressible wit who plunged himself, time and again, from one fit of laughter into another—the undying Proteus spirit which invariably returned in a new form and with new hopes. Ibsen's "Hollander" friends did not hesitate a minute in recognizing Vinje in Peer Gynt, and Ibsen had indeed utilized in his new Norwegian hero a special characteristic of Vinje's: the childish self-delight which appeared in his frequent quoting of his own remarks and verses.

Thus many things and many persons were mingled to form Peer the Norwegian; and everything could indeed be combined into one single personality because its life proceeded from genuine Norwegian imagination, from the Norwegian folk lore. During the time that Peer Gynt was taking form in Ibsen's imagination, the author veritably lived in the world of Norwegian legend, and the drama of Peer came to teem and swarm with subjects and traits from all sorts of fairy tales and legends, seldom so that they are palpably taken from one tale or another, nearly always so that they have given impetus to new growth and new creation in the author's mind. All this had not only the effect of making Peer deeply and intimately Norwegian, but it filled the drama about him with a brilliance and sparkle of fresh, playful poetry to which there is no equal in any other of Ibsen's works.

He was unusually high-spirited and happy, indeed exhilarated, at the time that he wrote *Peer Gynt*. It was at Christmas time in 1866, or at the beginning of the new year, 1867, that the new drama became clear to him and took on a firm outline; and he began immediately the work of planning and constructing. He expected to have it finished early in the summer. But even then he wrote: "It grows while in preparation"; and indeed he was barely able to put the first two acts into somewhat satisfactory form during the first four or five months. It was still a period of ferment and growth. But when a part of May had passed, and the heat of summer had come into the air, he left Rome and settled on the island of Ischia outside of Naples. There he lived for three months in the little town of Casamicciola, on the north side of the island, close beneath the old volcano, Epomeo; and here he was able to complete the first three acts of *Peer Gynt* and to make considerable progress with the last two.

It proved to be an exceedingly hot summer; but Ibsen worked as well as ever, despite the heat. It became evident now, and he was often to experience it later, that summer was the best working time for him. The heat which left other people wilted and exhausted, so that they could hardly force themselves to do